BEST OF IRISH
SOUPS

DELICIOUS MODERN RECIPES

Best of
Irish

BASED ON TRADITIONAL IRISH COOKING

EILEEN O'DRISCOLL combines a love of cooking with an awareness of the health and lifestyle benefits of good food, evidenced by the nutritional tips and information scattered throughout this book. A chartered physiotherapist and acupuncturist, she combines her busy Dublin practice with caring for her three children. She is the current president of the Zonta Club of Dublin, an international women's organisation founded in 1919 in Buffalo, New York, which promotes the political, legal, educational and social status of women. She has collected recipes from all over Ireland over the years and has attended cookery courses run by some of Ireland's leading chefs, including Gerry Galvin of Drimcong House. This is her first book.

Best of
Irish
Soups

EILEEN O'DRISCOLL

THE O'BRIEN PRESS

DUBLIN

First published 2002 by The O'Brien Press Ltd,
12 Terenure Road East, Rathgar, Dublin 6, Ireland.
Tel: +353 1 4923333; Fax: +353 1 4922777
E-mail: books@obrien.ie
Website: www.obrien.ie
Reprinted 2003, 2005, 2007.

ISBN: 978-0-86278-760-8

British Library Cataloguing-in-Publication Data.
O'Driscoll, Eileen
Best of Irish soups
1.Soups - Ireland 2.Cookery, Irish
I.Title II.O'Hara, Anne III.Irish soups
641.8'13'09415

4 5 6 7 8 9 10 11
07 08 09 10

Typesetting, editing, layout and design: The O'Brien Press Ltd
Author photograph: Christopher Dowley
Internal illustrations: Anne O'Hara
Cover photography: Walter Pfeiffer
Printing: Cox & Wyman Ltd

Contents

Introduction

Soup has been part of the Irish diet for generations, and is a natural choice given the abundance of vegetables, high-quality meats and the delicious harvest from our rivers and seas, as well as the wild bounty from our fields and hedgerows. Soup-making is a wonderful way of packing really good ingredients into one bowl to create a great starter, or indeed a complete meal with the addition of good bread. And, of course, in a time when many of us are more conscious of eating low-fat foods, consuming lots of vegetables and keeping body weight under control, soup is an ideal choice – low in calories and fat, high in nutrients and satisfyingly filling, so that the temptation to reach for the biscuit barrel is more easily resisted! Artful parents will also know that soup is a way of getting all that vital nutrition into children who will happily eat soup but would push away those same vegetables from their dinner plates.

The soups in this book will take you on a journey around some of the most beautiful spots in Ireland, from the Wicklow Mountains, which are the inspiration for a hearty onion soup, to Baltimore in West Cork, home of some excellent seafood. You will travel through County Tipperary, location of the famous Rock of Cashel and Devil's Bit Mountain and arrive in County Clare for Liscannor Rabbit Soup and a meeting with Máire Rua of the many husbands. Not too far to the north, the men of Aran are remembered for their beautiful black currachs with a tasty mussel soup. You will savour the fresh green taste of Patriot Soup and make the acquaintance of the Wild Salmon, Wild Garlic and domesticated Smoked Bacon and Pea soup.

Ideally, to make really great soup you should start with your own home-made stock. Many people shy away from making stock, thinking it too troublesome, but really it is very straightforward and once done can be repeated over and over with all your own additions and variations. You will find recipes for all the stocks you need in this book. However, there is a wide range of stock cubes now available which can be used instead. Look for organic stock cubes or low-salt cubes, as many brands are very salty and have monosodium glutamate added, so these should not be your first choice – check the list of ingredients.

With imports and all-year-round availability of most vegetables and fruits, there is a much wider choice of ingredients now than would have been at the disposal of the Irish cook years ago and these are reflected in recipes such as Roast Plum and Red Cabbage and Creamy Courgette and Tomato, but many of the old favourites, like Leek and Potato, Old-fashioned Pea and Wholesome Winter Vegetable, still taste as good as ever and will prove enduringly popular.

Versatile, quick and easy to make, soup can be served steaming hot on a cold winter's day or chilled for a delicious summer picnic. As a starter, main course, lunch or supper, creamy or low-fat, vegetarian or meaty there is absolutely nothing to beat a good soup. Try it!

For your added enjoyment, and to provide the perfect accompaniment to your home-made soup, I have included recipes for a range of breads and scones, including Ireland's famous wholemeal brown bread.

As seasoning is a matter of taste, I have not specified salt and pepper in any of the recipes. Use sea salt where possible, and freshly ground black pepper.

Butter has been used in all the recipes in this book. You may substitute olive oil in all cases; 1-2 tablespoons will suit most recipes.

V   **Indicates that the soup is suitable for vegetarians**

C   **Indicates that the soup can be served chilled.**

Boil: liquid is boiling when sufficient bubbles break the surface to cause it to roll.

Bunch of herbs (also known as a *bouquet garni*): usually means a few sprigs of parsley and thyme, with sage if desired or a bay leaf. Herbs such as rosemary, tarragon and fennel have powerful flavours and should be used to personal taste only.

Process: to purée or liquidise in a food processor/liquidiser/blender. A hand-held blender is ideal for soups as it can be used directly in the soup pot without having to transfer the soup to a processor.

Reduce: to shrink the quantity of liquid by rapid boiling, with the pot uncovered. Also intensifies the flavour.

Simmer: reduce the heat to stop boiling. Soup that is simmering will emit small bubbles, usually around the edge of the liquid.

Sweat: cook (in melted butter or oil) over a low heat for 1-2 minutes.

Toss: turn over several times with a cooking implement.

Stock

STOCK

To make stock, start with the right equipment. This will not break the bank and will allow you to make stock quite easily. You will need:

- I large pot
- I large strainer/colander with small holes
- I sieve

Quite large quantities of water are required to cover the stockpot ingredients, so the bigger and deeper the pot the better. I use a 7 ltrs/12¼ pts capacity pot for beef and turkey stock. I have a smaller stock pot, 3½ ltrs/5½ pts, for making vegetable stock and for using left-over roast chicken bones (Chicken Stock II). However, because there is so much liquid at the start, sometimes you need to reduce the stock at the end of the cooking time to increase the flavour. You can reduce the stock, ie decrease the quantity of liquid, by rapid boiling (and lots of steam in the kitchen) and in this way you can 'shrink' the amount of stock you have made and thereby increase the flavour.

Another important part of stock-making is skimming. This involves removing the scum that bubbles up to the surface when the stock comes to the boil initially and that continues to come to the surface during the cooking time. A large spoon in a cup or on a plate kept by your cooker is an invaluable tool for this purpose. Careful skimming will ensure that your stock is as clear as possible. At the end of the cooking time it is possible to clear it further to make what the French have called consommé.

When the stock is finished you will find a variety of results, from a quite mild taste, as in some vegetable stocks (not all), to a much richer flavour, as in chicken or beef stock. You will hear people tell you that you can 'throw anything' into a stockpot, but this isn't really true. Some ingredients are cornerstones of the stock, eg, onions and herbs like parsley and thyme, while some just take over and dominate the overall result, a bit like banana in a fruit salad. So be careful initially until you're sure. As a general rule, the better the stock flavour the better the soup.

BEEF STOCK

Ingredients:

2-2½ kg/5-6 lbs beef bones

225 g/8 oz carrots, cut into chunks

110 g/4 oz celery, sliced

454 g/1 lb onions, sliced

30 g/1 oz (or a good bunch of) parsley, thyme and other herbs, such as oregano and basil

2 bay leaves

13 peppercorns (for luck!)

water to cover (4-6.5 ltrs/7-10 pts/16-25 cups)

Method:

Place the raw beef bones in a roasting tin and brown them in a hot oven 200°C/400°F/Gas 6 for 30 minutes. Add the carrots, celery and onion to the tin and toss them around with the bones. Return to the oven for a further 15-20 minutes until the vegetables are changing colour to a more 'roasted' look.

Put all the bones and vegetables into a deep stockpot with the other ingredients. Bring to the boil and skim. Cover and simmer for 3 hours, skimming carefully throughout the cooking time. Strain and leave to cool.

When the stock is cold remove the fat from the surface. Because the fat solidifies and floats to the surface it is then easily removed with a slotted spoon. The stock is now ready to use.

Cook's Tip:

Always taste your stock for flavour and, if it is too weak, remember that you can concentrate the flavour by reducing the stock through rapid boiling in an uncovered pot.

chicken stock 1

This is a great recipe to start with, as you get stock plus a cooked chicken, which you can use hot or cold in a variety of ways. If you take the chicken meat off the bones when it is cooked you can add the bones back to the stock for a truly delicious result.

Ingredients:

1 x 1½ kg/3½ lb chicken

110 g/4 oz carrots, sliced

1 onion (as above), sliced

1 stick of celery

bunch of parsley stalks

1 bay leaf

sprig of thyme (optional)

6-8 peppercorns

water to cover (4 ltrs/7 pts/16 cups)

Method:

Place all the ingredients in the pot and bring to the boil. Skim the foaming froth off the top. Reduce the heat, cover and simmer for 1½ hours. Skim the surface a few more times during the cooking. Then remove the chicken from the liquid.

At this stage it is really easy to take the meat off the bones to use as you wish.*

Put the bones back into the liquid and cook for a further 1½ hours. Strain through a colander.

Taste the stock. If it is weak in flavour reduce it by a quarter of its volume.

This is now ready to be used in all your soup recipes, but is especially good with chicken soups.

* Such as in Nutty Party Chicken, p.79

Chicken Stock II

Ingredients:

1 roast chicken carcass

110 g/4 oz onions, quartered

110 g/4 oz carrots, cut into chunks

1 stick celery, cut into chunks

bunch of parsley

sprig of thyme

6-8 black peppercorns

1 bay leaf

water to cover (3 ltrs/5¼ pts/12 cups)

Method:

Place all the ingredients in a large pot, approximately 3½ ltrs/5½ pts capacity. Bring to the boil and skim off the froth/scum. Lower the heat, cover and simmer for 2½ hours, continuing to skim from time to time. Strain through a colander and cool. This is now ready to use or may be frozen for later use.

Chicken Stock III

This is serious chicken stock and makes an absolutely gorgeous base for sauces, soups and any dish requiring stock. Most butchers will have chicken bones left over from removing chicken breasts, so don't be afraid to ask. They nearly always have chicken necks as well, which were invented for soup! This stock is so good it's worth making a large amount and freezing it in smaller quantities. Use the large stockpot for this. Sometimes it's difficult to get giblets, so if you do find some buy extra for freezing.

Ingredients:

1¾-2 kg/4½-5 lb raw chicken bones and giblets*

450 g/1 lb onions, roughly chopped

225 g/½ lb carrots, chopped

4 celery sticks (90 g/3 oz), sliced

1 bay leaf

good bunch of fresh herbs, eg, parsley, thyme

8-10 peppercorns

water to cover (4-5 ltrs/ 7-8¾ pts/16-20 cups)

* the neck, gizzard, liver and heart of a chicken or turkey. May also comprise head, feet, cock's comb and kidneys. However, the livers of geese and ducks are not considered giblets.

Method:

Place all the ingredients in a large, deep pot. (I use a 7 ltrs/12¼ pts one.)

Bring to the boil and skim all the froth off. Lower the heat, cover and simmer for 3 hours. Continue to skim during the cooking time. Leave to cool completely.

When cold, strain through a colander. The stock is now ready to use or freeze.

fish stock

Fish stock is the quickest stock to make and very rewarding. White fish bones (cod, plaice, whiting, haddock or other white fish) are best for making stock. Don't use oily fish like salmon and mackerel as they will make the stock bitter. You can also use fish heads if you wash them well first – they add extra flavour. But don't use the skin or heads if you want a clear fish stock. Your local fishmonger is usually happy to provide bones. As this stock has a very short cooking time, the vegetables need to be finely chopped to allow them to release their flavour quickly.

Ingredients:

1¼ kg/3 lbs white fish bones

110 g/4 oz leeks, white part only, washed and sliced

110 g/4 oz onions, finely chopped

55 g/2 oz celery, finely chopped

30 g/1 oz dill

1 bay leaf

600 ml/1 pt white wine

juice of one lemon

10 peppercorns

30 g/1 oz/¼ stick butter

water to cover (3.6 ltrs/6 pts/14 cups)

Method:

Soften the vegetables in butter without allowing them to brown. Add the fish bones and toss with the vegetables for 1 minute. Add the wine and bring to the boil. Cook at a foaming boil for 2-3 minutes. Add the water, lemon juice and peppercorns and bring back to the boil. Lower heat, cover and simmer for 30 minutes. Skim regularly during the cooking time.

If the stock tastes too weak, reduce the quantity by a quarter to a third by rapid boiling, uncovered. Strain the stock and use for soups or sauces, or freeze for later use.

Cook's Tip:

If using for a sauce you can add a few drops of anchovy essence to get a really fishy taste.

Prawn shells roasted at 180°C/350°F/Gas 4 for 15 minutes will add an interesting flavour to your stock.

GAME STOCK

Make as for Chicken Stock II, using the carcass of pheasant or duck.

HAM STOCK

A 'feed' of bacon and cabbage was one of the stalwarts of Irish cooking for many years, but ham, being more expensive, was usually reserved for special occasions, and even then, nothing was wasted. The water in which the ham was cooked was never thrown out but used for making soups such as Pea and Ham Soup. So this is a double-value recipe, being one way to cook a ham and also the way to make ham stock.

Boiling a ham often gives a better result than baking, imparting more succulence and flavour to the meat. Do soak the ham in cold water overnight to get rid of some of the salt used in curing it.

Ingredients:

1.625 kg/3½ lbs ham fillet, boned and rolled. You can also use bacon

110 g/4 oz carrots

110 g/4 oz onions

55 g/2 oz celery

13 peppercorns

1 bay leaf

a few stalks of parsley

water to cover (4 ltrs/ 7 pts/16 cups)

Method:

Place the ham in a deep pot with all the other ingredients and cover with fresh cold water. Bring to the boil and skim off the froth. Cover and simmer (allowing 30 minutes to the ½ kg/1 lb) for 1¾ hours. When the ham is cooked, turn off the heat and leave it to rest for 10 minutes. Remove and serve hot or cold.

Strain the stock and allow it to get completely cold. It is then very easy to remove the fat from the surface. I usually measure the amount of stock left and reduce it (by rapid boiling, uncovered) to 2 ltrs/3½ pts if it is more than that.

VEGETABLE STOCK 1

This has to be the very best and easiest way to use all those vegetable pieces you normally throw away: ends of cucumbers and peppers, tomato cores, 'stringy' celery stalks, stumps of carrot and cauliflower and onion ends. Look at the ingredients below, which were the cast-offs of the steamed vegetables and a mixed salad (recipe p.78) which had accompanied a roast free-range chicken and potato bread!

Ingredients:

2 onion ends (1¼ cm/½ inch thick pieces cut off each end, with skins

2 red pepper ends, stalk removed

2 ends of one cucumber

2 sticks celery – very stringy outer stalks

stump of cauliflower, no green leaves

stump of iceberg lettuce

4 carrot ends

6 tomato cores and stumps

basil stalks

bay leaf

13 peppercorns

water to cover (1¼ ltrs/2 pts/5 cups)

Method:

Put all the ingredients in a stockpot. Bring to the boil and skim off the froth. Cover and simmer for 30-40 minutes. Strain and use or freeze.

For a stronger flavour, reduce the liquid by boiling rapidly, uncovered.

VEGETABLE STOCK II

Ingredients:

2 carrots (170 g/6 oz), scrubbed and chopped

5 onions (1 lb/½ kg), peeled and chopped

2 leeks, washed and sliced

2 celery stalks (85 g/3 oz), washed and chopped

6 cloves of garlic, crushed

13 peppercorns

55 g/2 oz/½ stick butter

55-85 g/2-3 oz fresh herbs, eg, parsley, thyme, bay leaf, basil

1.8-3.5 ltrs/3-4 pts/7¼-13 cups water

Method:

Sweat the vegetables, garlic and peppercorns in the butter over a low heat for about 3 minutes. Stir constantly and do not allow them to brown.

Cover the vegetables with the cold water and bring to the boil. Skim off the froth, cover and simmer for 30 minutes. Add the herbs and simmer for 2-3 minutes more. Strain the stock, taste for flavour and use or freeze.

Soups

BALTIMORE FISHERMAN'S SOUP

The lovely little harbour and village of Baltimore nestles on the coast of southwest Cork. This area is the ancestral home of the O'Driscoll clan who were seafarers and traders and felt free to indulge in a spot of piracy in their home waters, as the mood took them! On the quayside in the evenings you can see the fishermen arriving with their catch, unloading and preparing it for sale.

SERVES 4–6

Ingredients:

¾ kg/1½ lbs white fish, skinned and cut into cubes

½ kg/l lb mixed prawns, mussels and scallops

225 g/8 oz carrots, diced

110 g/4 oz onions, diced

340 g/12 oz potatoes, diced

bunch of herbs: dill and parsley, thyme and bay leaf tied together in muslin

30 g/1 oz/¼ stick butter

30 g/1 oz plain flour

600 ml/1 pt/2½ cups fish stock

300 ml/½ pt/1¼ cups milk

150 ml/¼ pt/⅔ cup cream

Garnish:

sprigs of dill

Method:

Melt the butter over a low heat and cook the onions until they are soft but not brown. Stir in the flour. Gradually add the fish stock, stirring constantly. Add the carrots, potatoes, milk and herbs and bring to the boil. Cover and reduce to simmer for 5-6 minutes. Check that the potato is cooked by prodding with a sharp knife. It should still be firm but the tip of the knife will slide into it a little. Don't allow the potato to get mushy.

Add the white fish and cook for 3-4 minutes over a low heat. Add the shellfish and bring to the boil. Remove from the heat, discard the herbs and add the cream. This helps to slow down the cooking as the fish continues to cook off the heat. Be careful not to overcook fish; the fish pieces should hold their shape but just begin to flake when tested with a knife.

Garnish with feathery sprigs of dill and serve with home-made brown bread.

BARLEY BROTH

Traditionally this broth was made with a piece of mutton on the bone, but this recipe uses home-made beef stock. Pot barley is preferable to pearl barley as pearl has had its outer hull, and therefore its nutrients, removed. Barley is another of the slow-burning carbohydrates, like brown bread, beans and pulses, which is filling and sustaining, particularly before a long walk on a cold winter's day. This soup is quick, easy and nutritious.

SERVES 4–6

Ingredients:

45 g/1½ oz pot barley, soaked in water overnight

110 g/4 oz each onions, celery, carrots and turnips, very finely diced

1 ltr/1¾ pts/4 cups home-made beef stock

bunch of herbs, thyme, parsley, bay leaf, tied together

Garnish:

chopped fresh herbs

Method:

Drain off the water from the barley.

Place the barley, stock and all other ingredients in a soup pot and bring to the boil. Cover and reduce to simmer for 30 minutes. Remove the bunch of herbs.

Garnish with a sprinkling of chopped fresh herbs.

Cook's Tip:

Barley contains soluble fibre, useful in maintaining a healthy gut and reducing blood cholesterol. It is also rich in minerals and a good source of iron and protein.

BEEF BROTH

This is one of the greatest recipes there is and makes a very sophisticated clear soup —
what the French call consommé. Although it takes a long time, the finished product, a
lovely amber colour, is well worth the effort. You can also add very thinly sliced fresh
vegetables to make a light but very nutritious soup.

SERVES 6–8

Ingredients:

2½ lbs/1 kg shin beef

1 lb/½ kg onions, cut in half

3 carrots (10 oz/300 g) whole, scrubbed

2 stalks celery (5 oz) whole, washed

1 leek, white part only, washed

13 peppercorns

1 bay leaf

parsley, thyme, chervil, basil

2 egg whites

2.7 ltrs/4-4½ pts/17 cups cold water

salt, to taste

Method:

Cut the meat into cubes and put into the cold water together with all the other ingredients except the egg whites. Bring to the boil, cover and simmer for 5-6 hours. Skim off any scum that forms on the surface. Strain through a fine sieve. You will get a clearer soup if you put a piece of muslin or fine cheesecloth over the sieve. Put the strained soup into a clean saucepan. Add the 2 egg whites and whisk them briskly while the soup comes to the boil. Stop whisking and reduce to simmer for 30 minutes. A crust will form on the surface, which you can push back with a spoon while you strain the soup once more through a clean cloth and sieve. Season to taste.

Broccoli and Apple Soup

The constituents of this simple soup are in abundance all year round. It is one of the quickest and easiest to make and so can be produced at very short notice indeed. It tastes equally well made with chicken or vegetable stock, so is a good choice for vegetarians. It is also excellent chilled and with its attractive light green colour, topped with golden toasted flaked almonds, it looks mouth-wateringly delicious.

SERVES 4–6

Ingredients:

225 g/8 oz eating apples, peeled and cored

340 g/12 oz broccoli (woody end of stem removed), roughly chopped

110 g/4 oz shallots diced

15 g/½ oz/⅛ stick butter

1 ltr/1¾ pts/4 cups chicken or vegetable stock

300 ml/½ pt/1¼ cups cream (optional)

Garnish:

toasted flaked almonds

Method:

Melt the butter and sweat the shallots over a moderate heat for about 2 minutes. Do not allow them to brown. Add the apples and broccoli and toss for about one minute. Pour in the stock and bring to the boil. Cover and simmer for just 15 minutes. Liquidise/process.

If using cream, add it now and heat the soup through without boiling.

For chilled soup, allow to cool completely and chill in the fridge.

Garnish with a sprinkling of flaked almonds that have been toasted until golden brown.

Cook's Tip:

If you don't have shallots you may use 55 g/2 oz onions instead.

 When made with vegetable stock.

CARROT AND DILLISK SOUP

Dillisk or Dulse is an edible seaweed with feathery purple fronds, very commonly found on Irish shores. The Irish name comes from duill meaning a leaf and uisce meaning water. This is a very attractive-looking soup with the purple colour of the dillisk contrasting with the orange of the carrot. The seaweed flavour is very subtle but it makes this an extremely nutritious and different soup. Seaweed is low in calories and high in mineral content: manganese, cobalt, chromium and selenium. It also contains calcium, magnesium and iodine. Nowadays, dillisk is usually bought dried in packets and is brought to life with a little soak in cold water.

SERVES 4–6

Ingredients:

454 g/1 lb carrots, scrubbed and sliced

225 g/8 oz onions, finely chopped

30 g/1 oz dillisk, softened in cold water for 30 minutes

110 g/4 oz potatoes, peeled and diced

900 ml/1½ pts/3¾ cups chicken stock

Method:

Put the carrots, onions and potatoes in a pot with the stock. Bring to the boil. Reduce heat, cover and simmer for 15 minutes. Process.

Meanwhile remove the dillisk from the water. Pat dry with a paper towel and snip with a scissors or chop with a sharp knife into very small pieces.

Add the dillisk to the soup mix and stir in thoroughly. Leave to cook for a further 5 minutes.

Serve with brown soda scones.

Cook's Tip:

Instead of dillisk use seaweeds like nori or kombu, the Japanese equivalent of kelp.

CARROT AND ORANGE SOUP

The O'Briens of Ireland are said to have descended from the famous chieftain, Brian Boru, who became High King of Ireland and defeated the Vikings at the celebrated Battle of Clontarf in 1014. Brian reputedly had a head of flaming red hair — more orange really — just like this glorious soup, which is a firm favourite in my home.

SERVES 4–6

Ingredients:

225 g/8 oz carrots, scrubbed and cut into chunks

110 g/4 oz onions, diced

170 g/6 oz potatoes, peeled and cut into big chunks

rind of 1 unwaxed orange, pared in one piece if possible (for easy removal at the end of cooking time)

1 ltr/1¾ pts/4 cups chicken stock

30 g/1 oz/¼ stick butter

Garnish:

1 tablesp chopped parsley

Method:

Soften the onion in the butter over a low heat for 3-4 minutes. Add the carrots and potatoes and toss for 1 minute. (You can omit this stage without major loss of flavour, in which case put all the ingredients with the stock into the soup pot and bring to the boil.) Add the orange rind and stock and bring to the boil. Reduce the heat, cover and simmer for 20 minutes. Remove the orange rind and process the soup.

Garnish with chopped parsley.

CARROT AND PARSNIP SOUP

This is comfort food at its best and an extremely simple soup to make. In spite of the arrival of Mediterranean influences, these root vegetables remain a great mainstay of the Irish diet and a carrot and parsnip mash would be a familiar vegetable combination to generations of Irish families. In this recipe the parsnip lends a touch of spice to complement the sweetness of the carrot. It's a very good winter soup, when carrots and parsnips are in plentiful supply.

SERVES 4–6

Ingredients:

340 g/12 oz carrots, scrubbed and sliced

110 g/4 oz parsnips, peeled and cut into thick chunks

170 g/6 oz onions, roughly chopped

1 ltr/1¾ pts/4 cups vegetable or chicken stock

1 tablesp lemon juice

Garnish:

rind of a quarter of a lemon, blanched in boiling water for 1 minute and very finely shredded

Method:

Put all the ingredients in a soup pot and bring to the boil. Cover and simmer for 20 minutes. Process and serve with a swirl of natural yoghurt topped with the very finely shredded lemon rind.

Cook's Tip:

For a richer taste you can add 150 ml/¼ pt/ ⅔ cup of double cream at the end of cooking time. Reheat the soup before serving, but do not allow to boil.

Add tofu, drained and chopped into cubes, to your vegetarian soups to make a main course meal or to add an extremely good supply of phytoestrogens.

Ⓥ When made with vegetable stock.

cauliflower soup

Simple, elegant and versatile, cauliflower soup is great hot or cold and very quick to make. For a special occasion, the addition of cream gives it a smooth, silky texture that is absolutely delicious. Like broccoli, cauliflower contains plant chemicals found to be benificial in the prevention of disease.

SERVES 4–6

Ingredients:

454 g/1 lb cauliflower, broken into florets

110 g/4 oz onions, chopped

110 g-170 g/4-6 oz potatoes, peeled and cut into chunks

1 ltr/1¾ pts/4 cups chicken stock

150 ml/¼ pt/⅔ cup cream (optional – for use in the smoother version, see 2. across)

Garnish:

croutons

Method:

Put all the ingredients (except the cream) into a pot and bring to the boil. Lower the heat, cover and simmer for 15 minutes.

There are two ways to serve this tasty soup:

1. Semi-processed, without cream and with pieces of cauliflower still visible in the soup. This gives a more 'rustic' look to the soup. Add a little extra stock if it's too thick.

2. Fully processed, with the addition of the cream. This gives a smoother, whiter soup. The soup will need to be reheated after adding cream, but do not allow to boil.

At the last second scatter a few crunchy croutons on top of each bowl to add that extra flavour and texture.

Cook's Tip:

To add a more exotic seasoning to mildly flavoured soups, try ground ginger or curry powder, which are also high in iron.

chicken broth

One of the best ways to use your own home-made chicken stock, this broth is light, nutritious and delicious. It also makes an elegant starter for a dinner party.

SERVES 4–6

Ingredients:

300 g/10 oz chicken fillet, skinned and sliced into thin strips

110 g/4 oz carrots, scrubbed and cut into matchsticks

110 g/4 oz onions, peeled and cut into sticks (see Cook's Tip)

55 g/2 oz turnips, peeled and cut into matchsticks

110 g/4 oz leeks, washed and cut into thin strips

110 g/4 oz parsley, finely chopped

1 ltr/1¾ pts/4 cups home-made chicken stock

30 g/1 oz/¼ stick butter

Method:

Melt the butter over a medium heat until foaming, add the chicken strips and toss until all the pink colour is gone. Remove from pot and set aside. Add all the vegetables and sweat them over a low heat for about 5 minutes. Do not brown. Add the stock and chicken and bring to the boil. Skim off any froth. Reduce the heat, cover and simmer for 30 minutes. Just before serving add the chopped parsley and cook for 1 minute.

Serve with crusty white bread.

Cook's Tip:

Onion Sticks

Slice the onion in half from root to tip, ie, lengthways. Divide these in two crossways, ie, across the width of the onion. Set each quarter on the cut side – the surface of the onion that was last in contact with the knife. Cut very thinly and you will find the onion will separate into 'sticks'.

Chicken Noodle Soup

A perennial favourite with children and adults alike. This soup must be used on the day it is made, otherwise the pasta swells in the liquid and takes over the soup completely. However, I've never had to deal with leftovers!

SERVES 4–6

Ingredients:

300 g/10 oz chicken breast, skinned and sliced into thin strips

110 g/4 oz onions, very finely diced

85 g/3 oz spaghetti, broken into 2½ cm/1 inch strips

1 ltr/1¾ pts/4 cups chicken stock

30 g/1 oz/¼ stick butter

30 g/1 oz plain flour

Garnish:

freshly chopped parsley

Method:

Soften the onion in the butter over a low heat without browning. This will take about 5 minutes. Add the chicken and cook until all the pink colour is gone.

Add the flour and cook for 1-2 minutes, stirring all the time. Now add the stock slowly, continuing to stir. Cover and reduce to simmer for 20 minutes. Increase the heat and add the pasta when bubbling. Cover and simmer until the pasta is cooked but still has a bite (*al dente*).

Serve in shallow soup dishes, which show off the texture of the soup. Sprinkle with freshly chopped parsley.

Cook's Tip:

You can make this soup the day before, omitting the pasta. Then when you are ready to eat it, reheat and add the pasta, as above.

chunky bean and vegetable soup

A hearty, filling, flavoursome soup that makes a meal in itself. Don't be afraid to experiment with other vegetables you may have rather than sticking slavishly to this recipe, although first time around you won't go wrong with this one.

SERVES 6–8

Ingredients:

225 g/8 oz haricot beans

170 g/6 oz each onions, carrots and celery, diced

3 cloves of garlic, peeled and crushed

110 g/4 oz chopped mixed fresh herbs (parsley, chervil, basil or coriander)

1.8 ltrs/3 pts/7½ cups vegetable stock

55 g/2 oz/½ stick butter

Garnish:

grated cheese or garlic baked breadcrumbs or chopped herbs

Method:

Put the haricot beans in a pot with the stock and bring to the boil. After 1 minute turn off the heat and leave to soak for 2 hours.

Meanwhile, in a soup pot soften the onions, carrots and celery in the butter over a low heat for about 10 minutes. Add the garlic and cook for another minute. Pour in the stock and add the beans and herbs. Bring the soup to the boil, reduce the heat, cover and simmer for about 1 hour. Take half of the soup and process it. Add back to the unprocessed soup, heat through and serve.

Garnish with grated cheese, chopped herbs or garlic baked breadcrumbs (see recipe p.75), or your own favourite topping.

CREAM OF CHICKEN SOUP

A great way of using up those inevitable pieces of leftover chicken, this soup is relatively quick to make. And if you are trying to cut down on fats, don't be put off by the title – it doesn't actually use cream!

SERVES 4–6

Ingredients:

454 g/1 lb cold cooked skinless chicken, chopped into small pieces

170 g/6 oz shallots (or 110 g/ 4 oz onions)

55 g/2 oz/½ stick butter

55 g/2 oz flour

600 ml/1 pt/2½ cups chicken stock

300 ml/½ pt/1¼ cups milk

150 ml/¼ pt/⅔ cup white wine

bunch of herbs in muslin (parsley and thyme, or simply tarragon)

Garnish:

chopped fresh herbs or croutons

Method:

Soften the shallots/onions in the butter over a low heat for 5 minutes, without browning. Add the flour and mix in well. Add the stock gradually, stirring constantly. Add the chicken, wine and bunch of herbs and bring to the boil. Cover and simmer for 15 minutes. Remove the herbs, add the milk and heat through without boiling. Process.

Sprinkle with chopped fresh herbs or crunchy croutons and serve with brown scones for a complete and delicious meal.

CREAM OF SMOKED HADDOCK SOUP

Another great fish soup that brings back memories of some glorious meals in the marvellous restaurants in the West of Ireland. Use real smoked haddock, not the dyed variety. It is really tasty and benefits hugely from the accompaniment of a glass of good Riesling ... so there!

SERVES 4–6

Ingredients:

170 g/6 oz undyed smoked haddock, cut into small chunks

110 g/4 oz onions, peeled and finely diced

170 g/6 oz carrots, scrubbed and finely diced

454 g/1 lb leeks, washed and finely chopped

150 ml/¼ pt/⅔ cup white wine

600 ml/1 pint/2½ cups home-made fish stock

55 g/2 oz/½ stick butter

30 g/1 oz flour

300 ml/½ pt/1¼ cups milk

Method:

Poach the smoked haddock in the milk over a very low heat until just beginning to flake. This doesn't take long (approximately 5 minutes from when the milk heats up). Set aside. Soften the vegetables in the butter over a low heat for about 10 minutes with the lid on – stir and turn over regularly. Now remove the lid and add the wine. Bring to the boil for 2 minutes, reduce the heat to low and add the flour. Cook for 2 minutes. Add the fish stock slowly, stirring constantly. Process. Strain if you want a very smooth soup.

Serve with a selection of breads.

Cook's Tip:

As the cooking time for the fish in this recipe is short, it is important to make sure that the vegetables are finely chopped. Over-cooking will destroy the flavour and texture of the fish.

CREAM OF SMOKED WILD SALMON SOUP

The salmon has a very important place in the folklore and diet of the Irish. One of the best-known legends about Fionn MacCumhail, leader of those mighty warriors, the Fianna, is 'The Salmon of Knowledge'. It was said that any man who tasted the flesh of this salmon would acquire great wisdom and foresight. Fionn, then a young boy, was cooking it for his master, under strict instructions not to taste the fish. A blister formed on the salmon's skin, Fionn pressed it down and in doing so burnt his thumb, which he immediately put in his mouth to ease the pain. Thus he gained all the knowledge and wisdom of the fish. Thereafter, when Fionn wanted to know something, all he had to do was suck his thumb!

Wisdom is not guaranteed with this soup, but it is a great way of using up the leftover pieces of a whole or half smoked salmon. Many people now use farmed salmon, but I think there is nothing to beat wild salmon for flavour and quality.

SERVES 4–6

Ingredients:

170 g/6 oz onions, diced

225 g/8 oz leeks, washed and chopped into small pieces

110 g/4 oz celery, thinly sliced

1 clove garlic

55 g/2 oz/½ stick butter

30 g/1 oz plain flour

1.2 ltrs/2 pts/5 cups fish stock

150 ml/ ¼ pt/⅔ cup white wine

110-170 g/4-6 oz smoked wild salmon pieces, very finely chopped

150 ml/¼ pt/⅔ cup cream

Method:

Sweat the vegetables in the melted butter over a low heat, stirring constantly without browning. Add the flour and cook for 2 minutes, again stirring all the time. Now add the stock little by little, stirring rapidly to prevent it sticking. When it is well blended, reduce the heat, cover and simmer for 15 minutes. Process and strain and return to a clean pot. Add the wine and bring to the boil for 2 minutes. Add the chopped smoked salmon and poach over a low heat for 5 minutes. Add the cream, reheat and season to taste.

This soup is delicious with a garnish of dill or parsley and served with nutty brown bread.

CREAMY COLCANNON SOUP

This soup is derived from one of the oldest dishes in Ireland, colcannon, which gets its name from the Irish cal meaning kale and ceann fionn meaning blonde or white-headed. And, indeed, the name accurately describes this dish of fluffy mashed potatoes mixed with onion and green kale. Kale is a type of cabbage that forms no compact head and has dark green, often curly leaves. Colcannon is traditionally eaten around Hallowe'en when kale is plentiful. Some people use green cabbage for this soup, but kale has a superior taste.

SERVES 6–8

Ingredients:

225 g/½ lb kale, chopped

675 g/1½ lbs potatoes, peeled and cut into small cubes

225 g/8 oz onions, diced

1½ ltrs/2½ pts/6 cups vegetable stock

55 g/2 oz/½ stick butter

300 ml/½ pt/1¼ cups milk

Method:

Melt the butter in a pan and add the onion, cooking gently for 5 minutes until the onion is soft but not brown. Add the kale and potatoes and cook for a further 2-3 minutes until the kale is beginning to wilt. Add the stock and bring to the boil. Cover and simmer for 15 minutes. Process and strain. Return to a clean pot and add the milk. Season well with sea salt and plenty of freshly ground black pepper to taste.

Serve with home-made brown scones.

CREAMY COURGETTE AND TOMATO SOUP

Equally tasty hot or chilled, this is an excellent soup for summer when the ingredients are in season. It has a luscious, fresh taste and is particularly good with garlic bread and as a prelude to chargrilled fish.

SERVES 6–8

Ingredients:

675 g/1½ lbs courgettes (zucchini), 'tailed' and chopped

454 g/1 lb fresh, ripe tomatoes, quartered

110 g/4 oz onions, roughly chopped

4 cloves of garlic, peeled and crushed

1 ltr/1¾ pts /4 cups vegetable or chicken stock

150 ml/¼ pt/ cup double cream

30 g/1 oz/¼ stick butter

Garnish:

garlic croutons

Method:

Over a moderate heat soften the onion in the butter for 5 minutes, without browning. Add the courgettes, garlic and fresh tomatoes and toss with the onion for about 2 minutes.

Next add the stock, bring to the boil, cover and simmer for 20 minutes. Process and, for a really smooth soup, strain through a sieve. (Leave out this stage if you like soup with 'bits' in it.) Add the cream and mix in well. Reheat but do not allow to boil.

Top with garlic croutons (see recipe p.75)

Cook's Tip:

Crushing garlic with the back of a broad-bladed knife or with a garlic press is the best way of releasing all its flavour quickly and completely.

 When made with vegetable stock.

CURRACh SOUP

Currachs are beautiful, black, low-sided rowing boats and were the traditional form of maritime transport off the west and southwest coasts of Ireland. My mother's first introduction to mussels was as a small girl in the 1920s visiting Connemara with her grandmother and seeing the tall men of the Aran Islands pulling nets of mussels from their boats – sleek and shiny black currachs. The black mussels looked like miniature versions of the currachs!

SERVES 6–8

Ingredients:

1 ¼ kg/3 lbs mussels

225 ml/8 fl oz/1 cup dry white wine

225 g/8 oz shallots or onions or spring onions, finely chopped

110 g/4 oz carrots, finely chopped

110 g/4 oz leeks, white part only

1 celery stalk

1 clove of garlic, crushed

small bunch of parsley, finely chopped

55 g/2 oz/½ stick butter

900 ml/1 ½ pts/3¾ cups fish stock

300 ml/½ pt/1 ¼ cups cream

Method:

Clean the mussels under cold water, discarding any that are not tightly closed. Scrape off adhering small shells or barnacles and remove the 'beards' – the small mesh of tough 'hair'.

In a wide-bottomed pot, heat the wine, half of the shallots/onions and the parsley. Add the mussels and cook over a high heat with the lid on until they are all open – this will take only 2-3 minutes. Shell all but 6 of the mussels and reserve the cooking liquid.

Heat the butter in a saucepan and soften the remaining onion, carrots, celery and leeks over a low heat, without browning, for about 10 minutes. Add the stock and the reserved mussel liquor and bring to the boil. Add the mussels and bring back to the boil. Cover and simmer for 10 minutes. Process and strain through a sieve. Return to a clean saucepan, add the cream and heat through.

For best effect serve in white bowls, placing one of the unshelled mussels in each. Be careful about seasoning as the mussels are salty.

GREEN SPLIT PEA AND DILLISK SOUP

This soup uses store-cupboard ingredients and so is a great standby dish. Beans, split peas, lentils and chick peas keep for months in jars and are excellent nutritionally. While beans usually have to soak overnight or for eight hours, split peas and lentils can be used straight away. The peas are full of protein and the dillisk adds extra minerals and vitamins.

SERVES 6–8

Ingredients:

454 g/1 lb green split peas, picked over and washed

225 g /8 oz onions, diced

170 g/6 oz carrots, scrubbed and sliced

55 g/2 oz celery, sliced

30 g/1 oz fresh herbs

1 clove of garlic, peeled and crushed

1½ ltrs/2½ pts/6 cups vegetable or chicken stock

30 g/1 oz dried dillisk

Method:

Soak the dillisk in cold water for 15 minutes. Drain off the water and chop the dillisk finely.

Place all the ingredients in a large pot and bring to the boil. Cover and simmer for 40-50 minutes. The split peas should be tender. Process. If the soup is too thick add extra stock or water.

Serve with potato bread for a filling, hearty meal.

Ⓥ When made with vegetable stock.

hearty red lentil soup

This is a very nutritious and colourful soup that makes use of store-cupboard ingredients. It is a very good source of phytoestrogens – plant oestrogens beneficial to both men and women. It makes a filling main course lunch soup after which if dinner doesn't come until tomorrow it doesn't seem to matter. It's also great for supper or any other time you need comfort food.

SERVES 4–6

Ingredients:

170 g/6 oz red lentils picked over*

170 g/6 oz onions, peeled and diced

110 g/4 oz carrots, scrubbed and diced

55 g/2 oz celery, diced

2 garlic cloves, crushed

1 x 400 g/14 oz tin of tomatoes

1½ ltrs/2½ pts/6 cups vegetable, chicken, or ham stock

4 slices smoked bacon cooked and cut into pieces (optional)

*this means checking through the lentils for bad ones or stones

Method:

Wash the lentils until the water runs clear, drain and add with the other ingredients to a soup pot and bring to the boil. Skim off the froth. Cover and simmer for 30 minutes. Remove half of the soup and process. Add back to the unprocessed soup and serve with brown bread.

V When made with vegetable stock, bacon omitted.

Leafy Lettuce and Spring Onion Soup

Leafy lettuce grows well in Irish soil and even the most amateur of gardeners can usually raise enough of a crop to sustain the kitchen through a summer of salads. This soup was invented for the more prolific vegetable gardeners who cannot eat their way through all their fine produce. While lettuce has a short life, the soup can be frozen and revived later to bring a taste of summer at any time of the year.

SERVES 4–6

Ingredients:

454 g/1 lb leafy green lettuce (not iceberg), washed well and roughly chopped

110 g/4 oz spring onions, cleaned and roughly chopped

170 g/6 oz potatoes, peeled and cut into small chunksd

55 g/2 oz celery, washed and sliced

900 ml/1½ pts/3¾ cups well-flavoured chicken stock

150 ml/¼ pt/⅔ cup cream

55 g/2 oz /½ stick butter

Method:

Soften the onions, lettuce and celery in the butter over a moderate heat for 5 minutes, taking care not to brown them. Add the potatoes and stock and bring to the boil. Cover and simmer for 15 minutes and then process and strain. Return to a clean pot, season and bring back to the boil. Add the cream and heat through but do not boil.

Serve with brown bread, or soda scones, and a glass of chilled stout.

Leek and potato soup

The leek may be the national emblem of Wales but it is also very popular in Ireland and easily grown. Its subtle taste gives a gorgeous flavour to this concoction. This soup can also be served chilled for an outdoor feast in summer. When chilled, leek and potato soup becomes the altogether more classy-sounding Vichyssoise!

SERVES 4–6

Ingredients:

454 g/1 lb leeks, washed and sliced

110 g/4oz onions, finely chopped

300 g/10 oz potatoes, peeled and cut into chunks

55 g/2oz/½ stick butter

900 ml/1½ pts/3¾ cups chicken stock

300 ml/½ pt/1¼ cups cream or milk, or extra stock if you prefer

Garnish:

freshly chopped parsley

Method:

Soften the leeks and onions in the butter over a moderate heat for 3-4 minutes, but do not brown. Add the potatoes, toss for a minute and add the stock. Bring to the boil, cover and simmer for 15 minutes. Process and add the *cream or milk. Heat through but do not boil.

Serve topped with very finely chopped fresh parsley and a swirl of whipped cream.

*If freezing do not add the cream.

Cook's Tip:

If you intend freezing a soup that has cream as an ingredient, do not add the cream until you have defrosted and reheated the soup and it is ready to serve. Otherwise you may get a very strong 'dairy' smell and taste which overpowers the flavour of the soup.

Liscannor Rabbit Soup

Rabbits were plentiful in Ireland at one time and were looked upon as the poor man's chicken. Many people still value them for their delicious taste and flavour. This recipe makes a tasty soup and provides juicy rabbit meat for adding to game pie. It has one very interesting ingredient, if you can get hold of it – poitín. Poitín is Ireland's famous, illegally distilled alcohol, made from cereal, usually barley. The clear, white spirit packs a mighty kick, by all accounts. There were many places around Ireland where one could find 'moonshine', not least in west County Clare where beautiful Liscannor looks out over the Atlantic Ocean.

SERVES 4–6

Ingredients:

1 young rabbit, divided into portions (ask the butcher to do this for you)

juice of one lemon

55 g/2 oz flour

85 g/3 oz/¾ stick butter

225 g/8 oz carrots, scrubbed and cut into chunks

225 g/8 oz onions, peeled and quartered

110 g/4 oz celery, cleaned and sliced into chunks

170 g/6 oz smoked rashers of bacon

1 bay leaf

bunch of parsley and thyme tied together

2 tablesp poitín or Irish whiskey (or use 150 ml/¼ pt/⅔ cup white wine)

water to cover (1.8 ltrs/3 pts/7½ cups approximately)

Garnish:

croutons

Method:

Soak the rabbit pieces in lemon juice and water in a single layer in a bowl. Leave for an hour and then drain and dry thoroughly with kitchen paper. Toss them in the flour.

Meanwhile, soften the vegetables in a deep pot with 55 g/2 oz/½ stick of the butter over a low heat for about 5 minutes, turning them over several times. In a separate pan, fry the bacon until the fat is crispy. Remove and chop or cut with a scissors into pieces. Reserve the pan fat. Add the remaining butter to the pan and toss the rabbit pieces in the hot fat until brown all over. Take care not to burn them, as the flour coating will get bitter. Add the rabbit and bacon to the vegetable pot with the herbs, water and whiskey and bring to the boil. Boil for 2 minutes. Cover and simmer for 1½ hours.

Remove the herbs and rabbit pieces and take the meat off the bones. Finely chop 55 g/2 oz of the meat. The remainder can be used for other dishes, such as rabbit pie. Measure the soup liquid and reduce it (by rapid boiling) or increase it (by adding water) to 1200 ml/2 pts. Process the soup and add the chopped rabbit meat.

Garnish with croutons and serve with a snifter of good Irish whiskey and some thick-cut brown soda bread.

máire Rua soup

Máire Rua, meaning Red Mary, (1615-1686) is a famous character in the history of County Clare. Many legends have grown around her – she was reputed to have married and murdered several husbands on their wedding night. Although this is untrue, she did have three husbands. This colourful beetroot soup is a real surprise to people who are familiar only with the vinegary taste of cold pickled beetroot. Fresh beetroot has a completely different, slightly sweet taste and produces a soup of a stunning dark pink/red hue. It's simplicity itself to make and is a great soup for Samhain (Hallowe'en), the ancient Celtic festival when witches gather, drink wine and eat red foods – the colour for love spells.

SERVES 4–6

Ingredients:

675 g/1½ lbs raw beetroot, peeled and diced

454 g/1 lb potatoes, peeled and quartered

225 g/8 oz onions, roughly chopped

110 g/4 oz carrots, chopped into small pieces

1¼ ltrs/2 pts/5 cups chicken (or vegetable) stock

Garnish:

natural yoghurt, chives (optional)

Method:

Put all the ingredients in a soup pot, bring to the boil and reduce to simmer for 20 minutes. Liquidise or process.

To bring out the colour of the soup, serve in deep white soup bowls and top with a swirl of Greek yoghurt, which can be dotted with chopped chives or left plain.

Cook's Tip

This soup should be eaten as soon as it's made, when it looks stunning. The colour and taste change on reheating. However, it is also very successful as a chilled soup.

Use gloves when preparing beetroot, as it has a strong red dye.

V When made with vegetable stock.

ϻOUNTAINY ONION SOUP

This is one for when the winter sun is low in the sky, particularly after a wind-blown walk in the Wicklow Mountains, which nestle close to the hills of South County Dublin. This soup can be made the day before as it never loses in reheating.

SERVES 6–8

Ingredients:

1½ kg/3½ lbs onions, peeled and sliced

110 g/4 oz/1 stick butter

1 teasp salt

1 tablesp plain flour

1½ ltrs/2½ pts/6 cups beef stock

300 ml/½ pt/1¼ cups white wine (optional)

1 bay leaf

1 bunch parsley, tied

sprig of thyme – tie up in a small piece of muslin or very worn, thin cotton

Garnish:

freshly chopped parsley, grated cheese, or croutons

Method:

Melt the butter over a low heat and add the sliced onion. Cook with the lid on for about 20-30 minutes. Do not allow to brown. Check and stir regularly. Remove the lid and add the flour. Cook for 2 minutes, mixing well. Meanwhile, heat the beef stock until it is warm but not steaming. Add it to the pot, stirring rapidly. Add the herbs and wine, and bring to the boil. Cover and simmer for 20 minutes. Remove the parsley, thyme and bay leaf. Process the soup (with a hand-held blender if you have one).

Serve in deep bowls and sprinkle with chopped parsley and grated cheese, or with home-made croutons.

Cook's Tip:

When using flour as a thickener, heat the liquid you are adding as it is less likely to form lumps.

OLÒ-ᚠASJIONEÒ PEA SOUP

This is a truly delicious soup and the thrifty cook has the added satisfaction of using up the water in which ham was cooked. Ham water is never wasted in Ireland and is appreciated for its excellent flavour. To give extra body and turn this into a main course soup, add any leftover ham pieces. Chicken or vegetable stock may be used instead of ham stock, but there is nothing to beat its special flavour in this recipe.

SERVES 4–6

Ingredients:

110 g/4 oz/1½ cups potatoes, peeled and cut into chunks

110 g/4 oz/1½ cups onions, peeled and chopped

675 g/1½ lbs frozen peas

1¼ ltrs/2 pts/5 cups ham stock

30 g/1 oz/¼ stick butter

Garnish:

natural yoghurt or cream, chopped mint or parsley

Method:

Melt the butter over a moderate heat and gently sweat the onion for 2 minutes. Add the potatoes and toss for 1 minute. Then add the peas (straight from frozen) and the ham stock. Bring to the boil, skim off the froth. Reduce the heat, cover and simmer for 15-20 minutes. Towards the end of the cooking time check the colour of the peas; they should still be very green. If they are showing any sign of yellow, remove from the heat immediately. Process.

Serve with a swirl of cream or yoghurt topped with a sprinkling of very finely chopped mint (or parsley if you don't have mint).

ONION BROTH

'There is, in every cook's opinion
No savoury dish without an onion
But lest your kissing should be spoilt
The onion must be thoroughly boiled' (Jonathan Swift)

Onions take second place after potatoes as the most commonly used vegetable in an Irish kitchen. This soup requires a large quantity of onions so the preparation can make you look like you've been watching a weepy film. The result is worth it though.

SERVES 4–6

Ingredients:

1½ kg/3 lbs onions, peeled, halved and sliced thinly

55 g/2 oz celery, finely chopped

110 g/4 oz/1 stick butter

55 g/2 oz flour

bunch of fresh herbs tied together (parsley, thyme)

1 ltr/1¾ pts/4 cups beef stock, heated (you can substitute chicken but beef is better)

Garnish:

grated cheese

Method:

In a large pot melt the butter and gently cook the sliced onions over a moderate heat until they turn a rich brown colour. Keep stirring and tossing them during this time and be careful that they don't burn. Add the celery and toss for 1-2 minutes. Stir in the flour and cook for 1-2 minutes. Do not allow it to stick to the pot. Add the heated stock gradually, stirring constantly. Add the herbs and bring to the boil. Cover and simmer for 20 minutes. Remove herbs.

Serve in deep bowls with fresh, crusty bread and pass around some grated cheese to sprinkle on top.

PATRIOT SOUP

If you are planning a St Patrick's Day brunch, what could be more appropriate than this beautiful green soup, topped with a swirl of cream and dusted with finely shredded carrot? You will also be doing your guests good as it is packed with vitamins and minerals, excellent for cleansing the digestive system and virtually fat free if you omit the butter and use vegetable stock. And it has been said to cure a hangover!

SERVES 4–6

Ingredients:

30 g/1 oz/2 tablesp chopped parsley and chives

110-170 g/4-6 oz chopped onions

1 medium courgette (zucchini), sliced

1 leek (green part only), washed and sliced

225 g/8 oz frozen peas*

2-3 leaves of green cabbage (eg, York), sliced thinly

1 ¼ ltrs/2 pts/5 cups chicken or vegetable stock

225 g/8 oz potatoes, peeled and chopped into chunks

30 g/1 oz/¼ stick butter

Garnish:

cream
finely shredded carrot

*This soup was made for frozen peas, which are excellent used in this way.

Method:

Gently sweat the onion and leek in the butter for about 2 minutes. (Leave out this stage for the low-fat version and put the onion and leek in with the other vegetables.) Add the stock and all the ingredients, excluding the peas and cabbage, and bring to the boil. Cover and simmer for 15 minutes. Then add the chopped cabbage and peas. Bring back to the boil. Cover and simmer for a further 5 minutes. Process.

Serve your lovely green soup in white bowls and top with a swirl of thickened cream, sprinkled with shredded carrot. Accompany with home-made brown bread or scones, or potato bread.

Cook's Tip:

The white part of the leek is delicious sliced, lightly cooked in olive oil or butter and added to mashed potatoes.

Variations:

With so many more vegetables available today, the modern cook may be tempted to add green pepper, mangetout and/or French beans as well as the listed ingredients, and perhaps basil or coriander instead of parsley. Just keep it green.

 When made with vegetable stock.

quick beetroot soup

This is a very quick, delicious and impressive soup, absolutely easy to make. Always use unpickled beetroot. You will find vacuum-packed, cooked beetroot in many supermarkets.

SERVES 4–6

Ingredients:

1 x 300 g/10 oz packet pre-cooked beetroot, cubed

1 x 400 g/14 oz tin tomatoes

2 garlic cloves, crushed

110 g/4 oz onions, roughly chopped

55 g/2 oz celery, roughly chopped

5 ml/1 teasp red wine vinegar

15 g/½ oz sugar

900 ml/1 ½ pts/3¾ cups chicken stock

30 g/1 oz /¼ stick butter

300 ml/½ pt/1 ¼ cups cream (optional)

Garnish:

grated carrot, or garlic croutons

Method:

Soften the onion and celery in the melted butter over a low heat for 3-4 minutes. Add the tomatoes and garlic and toss for 1 minute. Add the beetroot and the other ingredients, except the cream. Bring to the boil. Reduce the heat, cover and simmer for 15 minutes. Process.

If you are using cream add it now, reheat but do not boil. If not adding cream, just add a little more stock or water (150 ml/¼ pt/⅔ cup).

Garnish with grated carrot or garlic croutons.

RICh OXTAIL SOUP

This is a wonderful, flavourful recipe and surprising to those who haven't cooked an oxtail before. It is also very economical and freezes well. It takes a little more time than other soups but is well worth the wait. Oxtail stew was very popular in Ireland as a thrifty family meal and it still has fans in Italy, particularly in Tuscany where oxtail stew is a regional dish.

SERVES 4–6

Ingredients:

1 oxtail, trimmed of extra fat, washed, dried and cut into pieces

170 g/6 oz each carrots, onions, celery and turnip, very finely diced

900 ml/1½ pts/3¾ cups beef stock

55 g/2 oz/½ stick butter

30 g/1 oz plain flour

turnip

Method:

Put the oxtail pieces in the pot with the stock and bring to the boil. Reduce the heat, cover and simmer for 2 hours. Leave to cool completely. This is easiest done the day before you want it. When cooled, remove all the fat that will have come to the surface.

Strain the stock and remove the lean meat from the bones.

Sweat the vegetables in the butter for 10 minutes over a low heat with the lid on, stirring from time to time. Mix in the flour and cook for 2-3 minutes. Add the strained stock, having made up its volume to 1 ltr/1¾ pts/4 cups with the reserved oxtail meat. Bring to the boil and cook for 30 minutes. Remove half the soup to a blender or food processor and when smooth, add back to the soup in the pot. This is a very filling soup and can be a meal in itself served with some good bread.

ROAST PARSNIP AND GARLIC SOUP

This is a very comforting and uniquely flavoured soup. It is especially appetising on a damp, misty day in autumn or winter, but can also be chilled for a lovely summer soup. Ten cloves of garlic may seem a lot, but it becomes much softer and sweeter when roasted unpeeled. As garlic has antiviral and anticoagulant properties, it is worth adding to your diet in greater quantities.

SERVES 4–6

Ingredients:

10 cloves of garlic, unpeeled

300 g/10 oz parsnip, peeled and cut into 5 cm/2 inch chunks

110 g/4 oz chopped onions

110 g/4 oz potatoes, peeled and diced

1 ltr/1¾ pts/4 cups chicken stock

150 ml/¼ pt/⅔ cup dry white wine

a little olive oil

30 g/1 oz/¼ stick butter

Garnish:

natural yoghurt

rind of a quarter of an unwaxed lemon

Method:

Toss the parsnip and unpeeled garlic in a little olive oil and roast on a baking tray in a moderate oven, 180°C/375°F/Gas 4, for 30 minutes.

Meanwhile, soften the onion in the butter over a low heat. When the parsnip and garlic are ready put the garlic on a plate and, using a broad-bladed knife, squash the garlic cloves, squeezing the softened inner core from its outer covering. Put the parsnips and softened garlic in the pot with the onions and the diced potatoes. Add the stock and wine and bring to the boil for 2 minutes. Cover and simmer for 15 minutes. Process.

Serve with a swirl of natural yoghurt and very finely sliced lemon rind, which has been blanched in boiling water for 1 minute.

Cook's Tip:

Roasted garlic is great spread on toasted crusty bread, topped with cherry tomatoes and washed down by a fruity red wine.

ROAST PLUM AND
RED CABBAGE SOUP

This soup is inspired by the colours and fruits of autumn and has a slightly exotic taste that can be enhanced by dusting with a tiny pinch of cinnamon. Plums are plentiful in Ireland during August and September, but because of imports this soup can now be made all year round. In summer serve chilled for a delicious and different outdoor eating experience.

SERVES 4–6

Ingredients:

600 g/1¼ lbs plums (reduce the weight by a quarter if the plums are very sweet)

450 g/1 lb red cabbage, finely chopped

110 g/4 oz chopped shallots

110 g/4 oz carrots, cut into chunks

15 ml/1 tablesp red wine vinegar

15 g/½ oz/¼ stick butter

1¼ ltrs/2 pts/5 cups chicken stock

olive oil

300 ml/½ pt/1¼ cups cream (optional: if using cream reduce the amount of stock by that amount. I use cream only for the chilled version, but it's delicious either way)

Garnish:

cream

cinnamon

Method:

Rub a little olive oil on your hands and coat the plums with it. Place them on a non-stick baking sheet and roast for 30 minutes at 180°C/375°F/Gas 4. Meanwhile prepare the other ingredients. Melt the butter in a pot, add the chopped shallots and cook for 1-2 minutes. Add the carrots and cabbage and sweat them for about 2 minutes. When the plums are ready, chop them roughly, removing the stones but leaving the skins on.

Add the plums and stock to the vegetables in the pot and bring to the boil. Skim off any froth. Reduce the heat, cover and simmer for 30 minutes. Process and sieve.

If using cream, add at this stage and reheat but do not allow the soup to boil.

Garnish with a swirl of cream dusted with a pinch of cinnamon.

Cook's Tip:

The skins of the plums add to the nutrition content, colour and flavour of this soup and contain beta carotene, which is an antioxidant.

Rock of Cashel Soup

(Cashel Blue Cheese, Bacon and Roast Tomato)

The Rock of Cashel in County Tipperary is one of Ireland's must-see visitor attractions. An old story tells how the Rock was formed: the Devil, carrying in his mouth a huge chunk of rock that he had bitten off a mountain in Tipperary, was chased by a pack of Irish wolfhounds. As the hounds closed in on him, the Devil dropped his burden at Cashel, thus creating the famous spot. An unlikely story maybe, but to look at the Devil's Bit Mountain, near Templemore, against the horizon it does indeed seem as if a 'bite' has been taken out of it! The Cashel area is also home to the marvellous blue cheese used in this soup.

SERVES 4–6

Ingredients:

8 large tomatoes* or 1 x 400 g/14 oz tin tomatoes

170 g/6 oz streaky bacon (smoked, if possible)

55 g/2 oz /½ stick butter

55 g/2 oz /½ cup flour

170 g/6 oz onions, finely chopped

110 g/4 oz celery, finely chopped

55 g/2 oz carrots, finely chopped

1.2 ltrs/2 pts/5 cups chicken stock or vegetable stock, heated

300 g/10 oz Cashel Blue cheese, crumbled

150 ml/¼ pt/⅔ cup cream

a little olive oil

* for the best flavour, try to get the reddest and ripest tomatoes

Method:

Rub a little olive oil onto your hands and coat each tomato with it. Roast them in a hot oven 220°C/425°F /Gas 7, for about 30 minutes. Remove from the oven and process.

Fry the bacon slowly in a non-stick pan until the fat is crispy and then chop or break it into little pieces and set aside.

Reserve the melted bacon fat and use with the butter to cook the onion, carrot and celery over a low heat until the onion is softening. Add the flour and mix it in well with the butter and vegetables and cook for 1 minute. Pour in the heated stock, stirring constantly, and then the crumbled cheese and processed tomatoes.

Bring to the boil and cook for 1 minute. Allow to cool slightly and process. Add the cream and warm through, making sure not to bring it to the boil.

Serve in deep bowls and sprinkle with the reserved bacon bits.

Simply Celery and Tomato Soup

There's a lot going for this simple little soup: it's low-fat, vegan, diuretic, low calorie, anti-viral and tasty to boot! So you can feel quite virtuous while you are enjoying it, especially if you have used home-made stock, which is additive-free and less salted than commercial cubes.

SERVES 4–6

Ingredients:

454 g/1 lb celery, sliced into small pieces

225 g/8 oz onions, peeled and sliced

4 cloves of garlic, peeled and crushed

2 x 400 g/14 oz tins of tomatoes

900 ml/1½ pts/3¾ cups vegetable stock

freshly ground black pepper

Garnish:

chopped fresh herbs

Method:

Put all the ingredients into a soup pot and bring to the boil. Skim off any froth. Reduce the heat, cover and simmer for 20 minutes. Process and strain. Add pepper.

Serve in deep bowls and sprinkle with chopped fresh herbs. Excellent!

Cook's Tip:

Use celery hearts for salads and dips and keep the tougher outer stalks, particularly green ones, for soups and stocks.

SMOKED BACON AND BABY PEA SOUP

This recipe combines the traditional ingredients of ham and pea soup, but with a little difference. It's easy to store frozen peas and bacon will keep well in the fridge, so you can have delicious soup very easily indeed. Smoked bacon adds a particularly interesting flavour.

SERVES 4–6

Ingredients:

170 g/6 oz smoked rashers of bacon

225 g/8 oz frozen petit pois or baby peas (they're much sweeter than the bigger ones)

110 g/4 oz onions, finely chopped

1 ltr/1¾ pts/4 cups chicken stock (use ham stock if you have it)

1 tablesp finely chopped fresh mint

30 g/1 oz/¼ stick butter

Garnish:

cream

Method:

Fry the bacon in a non-stick pan until the fat is crispy. Remove from the pan (reserving the fat) and cut the bacon into very small pieces with a kitchen scissors or a knife. Add the butter to a soup pot with the reserved bacon fat and soften the onion for 3-4 minutes over a moderate heat. Do not brown. Next add the peas, straight from frozen, and half of the mint with the stock and chopped bacon. Bring to the boil, reduce the heat, cover and simmer for 15 minutes, maximum. Do not let the peas overcook. Check the colour and if they are changing from fresh green to a more yellowy green switch off immediately. The greener the peas the sweeter the taste; they can become a little bitter with overcooking.

Process, but leave the soup a little 'gritty' for a more chewy texture.

Serve with a swirl of cream and sprinkled with the remaining mint.

SORREL AND CHIVE SOUP

Sorrel is a herb that is in season in spring and early summer. It is a little keener and sharper in taste than spinach and grows happily in a corner of the garden if you keep it well watered. Its lively taste cleverly balances the other ingredients in this soup.

SERVES 4–6

Ingredients:

110 g/4 oz leeks, washed and sliced thinly

110 g/4 oz shallots or onions, diced

300 g/10 oz potatoes, peeled and cubed

1 tablesp chopped parsley

bunch of sorrel (55 g-110 g /2-4 oz), washed and chopped

85 g/3 oz chives, washed and snipped into small pieces – reserve one third of these for garnish

30 g/1 oz/¼ stick butter

900 ml/1½ pts/3¾ cups vegetable or chicken stock

Garnish:

cream or natural yoghurt

chives

Method:

Soften the leeks and shallots in the butter over a low heat. Add the sorrel and 55 g/ 2 oz chives and cook for a further 3 minutes. Next add the potatoes, parsley and stock and bring to the boil. Reduce the heat, cover and simmer for 15 minutes.

Process and serve topped with a swirl of cream or natural yoghurt and sprinkled with the remaining chives.

V When made with vegetable stock.

SPRING NETTLE AND SORREL SOUP

'Down by the glenside I met an old woman, A-plucking young nettles, she ne'er saw me comin' ('The Bould Fenian Men'). Nettles are found all over Ireland and were traditionally picked in spring when they were used as a post-winter tonic* to cleanse and purify the blood. They were also used as a vegetable before cabbage became common. An old saying advises you to 'grasp a nettle like a lad of mettle', in order to avoid being stung, but it's best to use gloves. * Nettles are a rich source of iron.

SERVES 4–6

Ingredients:

110 g/4 oz onions, finely chopped

300 g/10 oz leeks, washed and sliced thinly

55 g/2 oz celery, sliced thinly

300 g/10 oz nettles, washed and roughly chopped

110 g/4 oz sorrel, washed and chopped

340 g/12 oz potatoes, peeled and chopped

55 g/2 oz/½ stick butter

1 tablesp chopped parsley

½ bay leaf

900 ml/1½ pts/3¾ cups chicken stock

300 ml/½ pt/1¼ cups cream

Method:

Melt the butter over a low heat, add the onions, leek and celery and cook until soft. Add the potatoes, bay leaf and stock and bring to the boil. Cover and reduce to simmer for 15 minutes. Next add the nettles, sorrel and half of the parsley and cook for 5 minutes more. Process, sieve and return to a clean saucepan. Add the cream or milk and heat through but do not boil. Season to taste.

Serve with the remaining parsley sprinkled on top.

Cook's Tip:

Pick only the tips, and stick to young nettle plants, not the large, mature ones seen from May onwards.

Nettles

SUMMER TOMATO BROTH

This is made with lovely ripe Irish tomatoes, which are at their juiciest in late summer and can be had relatively cheaply by the box from a good vegetable shop. The soup can be frozen and stored for a little taste of summer in cooler autumn days, but is absolutely marvellous for a summer lunch with a delicious goats cheese tart to follow.

SERVES 4–6

Ingredients:

1 kg/2½ lbs fresh, ripe tomatoes, quartered

4 cloves garlic, crushed

1 large red pepper, cored, deseeded and diced

225 g/8 oz onions, peeled and chopped

110 g/4 oz carrots, scrubbed and diced

bunch of parsley and thyme tied together in muslin

900 ml/1½ pts/3¾ cups vegetable stock

150 ml/¼ pt/⅔ cup white wine

150 ml/¼ pt/⅔ cup freshly squeezed orange juice*

Garnish:

finely sliced orange rind

Method:

Put all the ingredients, except the orange juice, in a large pot and bring to the boil. Reduce the heat, cover and simmer for 20 minutes. Remove the herbs. Process and strain. Return to a clean pot, add the orange juice*(quantity depends on your taste; you may want to use less) and season with sea salt and freshly ground black pepper. If the orange juice is not sweet you can add 1 teaspoon of sugar to the broth and mix in well.

Serve chilled and garnish with finely sliced orange rind that has been blanched in boiling water for 1 minute.

Cook's Tip:

For a different, more 'herby' taste, omit the orange juice and add 55 g/2 oz of fresh basil just before processing.

WATERCRESS AND PARSLEY SOUP

Watercress was a staple food in Ireland until modern times and would have been the traditional partner to bacon before cabbage took over that role. It grows throughout the year and can be found where there is shallow running water, but nowadays only commercially grown watercress should be used in cooking. This soup is light, very easily made and very good for you, containing potassium, calcium and iron as well as beta carotene and vitamins C and E.

SERVES 4–6

Ingredients:

454 g/1 lb watercress, washed thoroughly and roughly chopped

170 g/6 oz potatoes, peeled and diced

110 g/4 oz leeks, washed and sliced

55 g/2 oz chopped parsley

55 g/2 oz/½ stick butter

900 ml/1½ pts/3¾ cups chicken or vegetable stock

300ml/½ pt/1¼ cups milk

Method:

Soften the watercress and leeks in the butter over a very low heat with the lid on for 10-15 minutes. Add the potatoes and the stock and bring to the boil. Reduce the heat, cover and simmer for 15 minutes. Process, strain and return to a clean pot. Add the milk and parsley (reserve a little for garnish) and season to taste.

Sprinkle with the remaining chopped parsley and serve with your delicious home-made potato bread.

V When made with vegetable stock.

wholesome winter vegetable soup

This is just what you need on a cold day in mid-winter to defrost frozen fingers and turn a blue nose pink again! To coin a phrase, 'there's eatin' and drinkin' in it', and with home-made brown bread it makes a complete meal.

SERVES 6–8

Ingredients:

225 g/8 oz potatoes, peeled and diced

110 g/4 oz turnip, peeled and diced

110 g/4 oz onions, diced

55 g/2 oz parsnip, peeled and cut into small chunks

170 g/6 oz carrots, scrubbed and diced

1 x 400 g/14 oz tin of tomatoes

1.25 ltrs/2 pts/5 cups vegetable or chicken stock

7 cloves of garlic, crushed

300mls/½ pt/1¼ cups cream or milk (optional)

Method:

Place all the ingredients, with the stock, in a large pot. Bring to the boil. Reduce the heat, cover and and simmer for 20 minutes. Using a slotted spoon, remove 2 ladles of vegetables from the soup and process the remainder. Add the unprocessed vegetables back to the pot. This gives the soup a lovely chunky texture.

If using cream or milk, add now and heat through without boiling.

Serve with thick-cut brown soda bread and steam your way to comfort and satisfaction!

🅥 When made with vegetable stock.

WILD GARLIC AND POTATO SOUP

The scent of wild garlic fills the warm summer air in the Irish countryside, particularly near well-established woods. It's easily gathered and will provide a treasure-trove of flavour on return from your walk, when you can make a quick and tasty soup. Wild garlic is green and leafy, with a head of small, white flowers, and has a much more subtle flavour than its more familiar domesticated cousin. Only the leaves are used in cooking.

SERVES 4–6

Ingredients:

30-55 g/1-2 oz/2-4 tablesp wild garlic, chopped

110 g/4 oz shallots, chopped

675 g/1½ lbs potatoes, peeled and quartered

900 ml/1½ pts/3¾ cups chicken stock

30 g/1 oz/¼ stick butter

Garnish:

chives

Method:

Gently sweat the shallots in the butter over a low heat for 2-3 minutes. This stage is optional as you can make a very low-fat soup without it, but it does add to the flavour. If you don't have shallots use ordinary onions but halve the amount (55 g/2 oz). Then add all the other ingredients and bring to the boil. Reduce the heat, cover and simmer for 20 minutes. Liquidise or process.

Garnish with chopped chives.

This is a lovely lunch soup and tastes even better eaten out of doors with crusty bread.

Cook's Tip:

To get a 'clean', sharp edge, snip chives with a scissors.

wilD mushroom soup

Wild field mushrooms can be found in abundance in August and September in Ireland, particularly in fields where sheep or horses have been grazing. They have a distinctive white, smooth cap about 2½ -7 cm/1-3 inch across. The gills start pink and gradually darken to chocolate brown, avoid mushrooms with white gills, as there are some toxic wild mushrooms. Mushrooms have a lot of flavour in their skins so wipe them with a clean cloth rather than peel them. It's worth the effort.

SERVES 4–6

Ingredients:

675 g/1½ lbs wild mushrooms, cleaned and chopped

225 g/8 oz leeks, washed and chopped

30 g/1 oz celery, chopped

900 ml/1½ pts/3¾ cups chicken stock

300 ml/½ pt/1¼ cups milk

bunch of fresh herbs, tied together

55 g/2 oz/½ stick butter

55 g/2 oz plain flour

Garnish:

cream or natural yoghurt

Method:

Soften the leek, celery, mushrooms and herbs in the butter over a low heat for 10 minutes. Add the flour and cook for 2 minutes. Meanwhile, heat the chicken stock until hot but not steaming. Add the heated chicken stock to the vegetables, stirring constantly while thickening. Bring to the boil. Add the the milk and heat through but do not boil. Remove the herbs and process the soup.

Serve with a swirl of thickened cream or natural yoghurt.

Breads

POTATO BREAD

Not only is potato bread delicious but it is a very clever way of using up leftover mashed or creamed potatoes.

Ingredients:

225 g/8 oz self-raising flour
½ teasp salt
55 g/2 oz/½ stick butter or margarine
225 g/8 oz mashed potatoes
1 large egg, beaten
a little milk

Method:

Preheat the oven to 190°C/375°F/Gas 5. Put the flour and salt into a bowl and mix in the fat with your fingertips. Rub in the potatoes, or use a fork if you prefer. Make a well in the centre and add the egg, and a little extra milk if necessary, to make a soft, pliable dough. Remove from the bowl and knead for a few minutes on a floured surface until smooth.

Roll out to 1 cm/½ inch thickness and cut into rounds 5 cm/2 inch in diameter. Keep gathering all the leftover bits together until all the dough is used up. Place on a baking tray and bake for 30 minutes until they are golden brown. To preserve a soft outer crust, cover the breads in a clean tea-towel until ready to eat.

Cook's Tip:

This recipe can be frozen at the dough stage. Place a round of parchment/greaseproof paper between each bread, making it easy to separate them when you are ready to bake. Bake straight from the freezer, adding a few minutes to the cooking time, if necessary.

TOMATO BREAD

This is a variation on soda bread. It has an attractive flavour and colour and can be prepared very quickly. If you are feeling energetic, you could make a quick soup while it is baking in the oven!

Ingredients:

454 g/1 lb plain white flour

1 teasp salt

1 teasp sugar

1 teasp bread soda/ bicarbonate of soda

1 tablesp tomato purée

30 g/1 oz sundried tomatoes, drained, dried and diced

400 ml/¾ pt/1¾ cups buttermilk (see buttermilk recipe p77)

Method:

Sift the dry ingredients together and add the chopped tomato pieces. Make a well in the centre and pour in the buttermilk, into which you have whipped the tomato purée. Mix to a soft dough.

Turn onto a floured surface and knead until smooth (2-3 minutes).

Shape into a circle about 4 cm/1½ inches deep. Take a sharp, well-floured knife and cut a deep cross in the top. Bake at 220°C/ 450°F/Gas 8 for 45 minutes. Tap the bottom to see if it sounds hollow and if not return it to the oven for another few minutes. Turn onto a wire rack to cool.

Cook's Tip:

For extra flavour add a teaspoon of dried basil.

White Soda Bread

Many Irish children have been lucky enough to enjoy freshly baked soda bread as part of their upbringing. It has to be the quickest way to make tasty bread and this recipe is versatile in that it can also be used for scones. With the addition of sugar and dried fruit you can provide a teatime treat as well.

Ingredients:

454 g/1 lb plain white flour
1 teasp salt
1 teasp sugar
1 teasp bread soda
400 mls/ ¾ pt/1¾ cups buttermilk (see buttermilk recipe p.77)

Method:

Pre-heat the oven to 220°C/450°F/Gas 8. Sift the dry ingredients into a large bowl and make a well in the centre. Add the buttermilk. (It's a good idea to reserve a little of the milk until you are sure that the dough will not be too wet). Mix to a soft dough. Turn onto a floured surface and knead for a few minutes until the dough is smooth. Shape into a circle about 4 cm/1½ inches deep. Take a sharp, well-floured knife and cut a deep cross in the top. Place on a baking sheet and bake for 30-35 minutes. Tap the bottom of the bread when cooked. It should sound hollow. Put on a wire rack to cool.

Scones:

To make scones, flatten the dough to about 1.25 cm/½ inch thick and cut into 5 cm/ 2 inch rounds. Bake in the oven at 220°C/ 450°F/Gas 8 for 10-15 minutes.

This recipe freezes well and defrosts quickly in scone form.

wholemeal brown bread

The staple food of many Irish homes to this day is brown bread, and there are as many recipes as there are cooks in Irish kitchens. Because the flour retains the outer husk and inner germ where all the nutrients are, it is far more beneficial to the system than ordinary white bread, which has had these bits removed. This recipe is easy to follow and you can experiment with adding wheatgerm or ground sunflower seeds or by substituting* soya flour or more white flour for a little of the wholemeal flour.

Ingredients:

340 g/12 oz wholemeal flour

110 g/4 oz pinhead oatmeal

2 teasp bread soda

1 teasp salt

300 ml/ ½ pt/1¼ cups buttermilk

* To substitute soya or white flour, start by replacing 30 g/1 oz wholemeal; you can get more adventurous as you progress. Adding 1-2 teasp wheatgerm or sunflower seeds gives extra nutrients and taste. Add a *little* extra buttermilk if the mix seems dry.

Method:

Mix all the dry ingredients in a bowl and make a well in the centre. Add enough milk to make a soft dough. Turn onto a lightly floured surface and knead for a few minutes until smooth with no cracks. Shape into a 20 cm/ 8 inch round. With a floured knife, cut a cross from edge to edge and bake at 200°C/400°F/Gas 6 for 30-35 minutes. Tap the bottom and you will hear a hollow sound when it's cooked. Turn onto a wire rack to cool.

As well as being the perfect partner to many of the soups in this book, this bread is delicious with smoked salmon or mackerel, cream cheese and a wide variety of savouries, but also comes into its own served with lashings of home-made blackberry jam – Yum!

garnishes

GARLIC BAKED BREADCRUMBS

Ingredients:

110 g/4 oz white bread,
(ends of loaves are perfect)

2 cloves garlic

2-3 tablesp olive oil

½ teasp salt

Method:

Crush the garlic, using a broad-bladed knife or garlic press. Add to the oil. Leave for about 30 minutes. In a food processor, lightly process the bread into gravel-sized crumbs. Don't make them too fine. Add the breadcrumbs and salt to the garlic oil and toss until they are well coated. Transfer to a baking sheet and cook for 5 to 10 minutes in a hot oven, 200°C/400°F/Gas 6 until golden brown and crispy.

GARLIC CROUTONS

Use the recipe above to make Garlic Croutons, but instead of processing the bread cut it into even-sized, small cubes.

EXTRAS

BUTTERMILK

If you can't buy buttermilk this recipe will make all you want. Because the recipe creates a culture, you can go on using it indefinitely, making sure that you rinse it in tepid water every 4-5 days. Do not use hot water, as it will kill the yeast.

Ingredients:

30 g/1 oz white sugar

30 g/1 oz yeast

1.2 ltrs/2 pts/5 cups tepid milk

1.2 ltrs/ 2 pts/5 cups tepid water

Method:

Mix the sugar and yeast. Gradually add the tepid milk and water. Cover and leave at room temperature for 2 days. You should get a sharp but pleasantly clean smell when it is ready. Strain the buttermilk and use for your soda bread. Keep the spongy residue that remains in the strainer. This is the culture and it can be used to make more buttermilk by rinsing it in tepid water and then adding more tepid water and milk to continue the process.

coco's salad

This simple salad created the leftovers for the Vegetable Stock recipe on p.20.

SERVES 6–8 AS A SIDE DISH

Ingredients:

2 small red onions, peeled
and very finely diced

2 red peppers, cored,
deseeded and finely diced

2 celery stalks from the pale
'heart', finely chopped

6 tomatoes, cored,
deseeded and finely
chopped

1 cucumber, sliced and
diced

Method:

Mix all the ingredients in a decorative bowl
and add a tablespoon of French dressing or
olive oil and balsamic vinegar.

Even people who don't like the individual
ingredients enjoy this salad because
everything is chopped so finely the tastes
blend better.

NUTTY PARTY CHICKEN

This is a very simple and easily made cold chicken dish, which is very popular at buffets. It is ideal for using up the boiled chicken from the Chicken Stock recipe on p.15.

SERVES 6–8

Ingredients:

meat of a cooked chicken, cold, skinned and boned

handful (approx 55 g/2 oz) toasted almonds, halved

45 ml/3 tablesp good quality mayonnaise (no sugar added)

15 ml/1 tablesp tomato ketchup

Method:

Break up the chicken into bite-sized pieces. Mix the mayonnaise and ketchup thoroughly. Add the chicken pieces and most of the almonds to the mayonnaise, reserving some almonds as a garnish. Arrange on an attractive serving plate.

- Tins of tomatoes are a great substitute for fresh ones out of season
- Sprinkling fresh nuts on your soup adds extra protein and minerals, especially brazil nuts, which are high in selenium – an important anti-oxidant.
- If you want to be a bit exotic, for extra seasoning add ground ginger or curry powder, which are also high in iron.
- Mussels are a good source of Vitamin B12, which you need for healthy blood.
- Cabbage, broccoli, cauliflower, onions and garlic are very beneficial to the respiratory system.
- Use celery hearts for salads and dips and keep the tougher outer stalks, particularly green ones, for soups and stocks.
- You can alter the texture of any soup by increasing or decreasing the amount of stock, water, milk or cream.
- Add tofu, drained and chopped into cubes, to your vegetarian soups to make a main course meal or to add an extremely good supply of phytoestrogens.
- You can leave out the butter in most of the soup recipes if you want to reduce your fat intake. Many soups will taste just as good. You can also use olive or vegetable oil if you prefer.
- Crushing garlic with the back of a broad-bladed knife or with a garlic press is the best way of releasing all its flavour quickly and completely.
- Use heavy-based saucepans for better cooking performance. Things don't burn as quickly on to their surfaces and they keep their heat for longer, which is more economical.